Fairy Tales

READY-TO-USE SCRAPBOOK PAGES

Paige Hill

Sterling Publishing Co., Inc. New York
A Sterling/Chapelle Book

Author: Paige Hill

If you have any questions or comments, please contact:
Chapelle, Ltd., Inc., P. O. Box 9252, Ogden, UT 84409
(801) 621-2777 • (801) 621-2788 Fax
e-mail: chapelle@chapelleltd.com
Web site: www.chapelleltd.com

Instant Memories is a trademark of Sterling Publishing Co., Inc.

PC Configuration: Windows 98 or later with 128 MB Ram or greater. At least 100 MB of free hard disk space. Dual speed or faster CD-ROM drive, and a 24-bit color monitor.

Macintosh Configuration: Mac OS 9 or later with 128 MB Ram or greater. At least 100 MB of free hard disk space. Dual speed or faster CD-ROM drive, and a 24-bit color monitor.

10 9 8 7 6 5 4 3 2 1
Published by Sterling Publishing Co., Inc.
387 Park Avenue South, New York, NY 10016
© 2005 by Sterling Publishing Co., Inc.
Distributed in Canada by Sterling Publishing
c/o Canadian Manda Group, 165 Dufferin Street
Toronto, Ontario, Canada M6K 3H6
Distributed in the United Kingdom by GMC Distribution Services,
Castle Place, 166 High Street, Lewes, East Sussex, England BN7 1XU
Distributed in Australia by Capricorn Link (Australia) Pty. Ltd.
P. O. Box 704, Windsor, NSW 2756, Australia
Printed and Bound in China
All Rights Reserved

Sterling ISBN-13: 978-1-4027-3050-4
        ISBN-10: 1-4027-3050-0

For information about custom editions, special sales, premium and corporate purchases, please contact Sterling Special Sales Department at 800-805-5489 or specialsales@sterlingpub.com.

Introduction

Scrapbooking is a wonderful way to document special day-to-day events, holidays, celebrations, and family history. However, not everyone has the time or the money to do what it takes to create show-stopping scrapbook pages. That's where the *Instant Memories Ready-to-Use Scrapbook Page* series comes in. The top designers in the field have done all the work for you—simply add your favorite photos to their layouts and you're done! Or add a few embellishments, such as a charm or ribbon, and you have a unique personalized page in minutes. You can tear the pages directly from the book, photocopy them to use time and again, or print them from the enclosed CD.

As an added bonus in the *Instant Memories* series, we have included hundreds of rare, vintage images on the enclosed CD-ROM. From Victorian postcards to hand-painted beautiful borders and frames, it would take years to acquire a collection like this. However, with this easy-to-use resource, you'll have them all right here, right now, to use for any computer project over and again. Each image has been reproduced to the highest quality standard for photocopying and scanning and can be reduced or enlarged to suit your needs.

Perfect for paper crafting, scrapbooking, and fabric transfers, *Instant Memories* books will inspire you to explore new avenues of creativity. We've included a sampling of ideas to get you started, but the best part is using your imagination to create your own projects. Be sure to look for other books in this series as we continue to search the markets for wonderful vintage images.

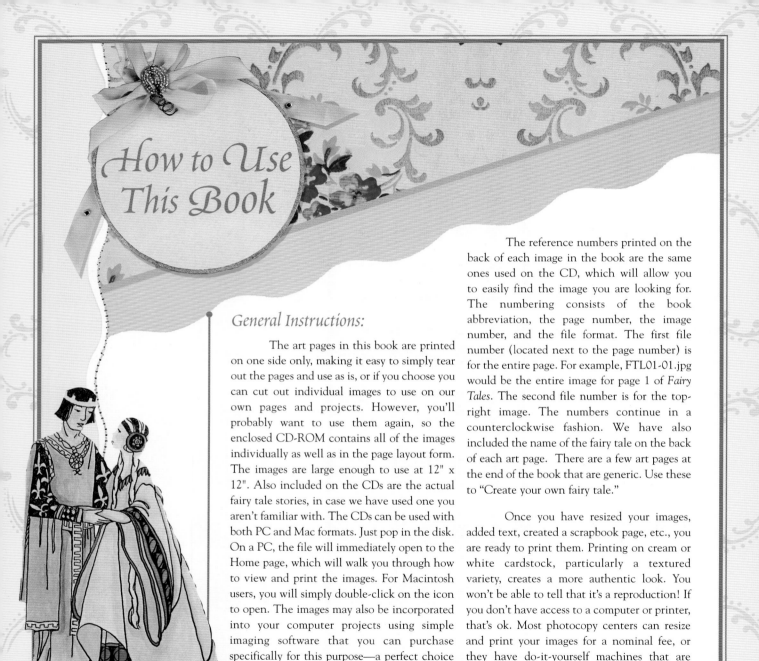

How to Use This Book

General Instructions:

The art pages in this book are printed on one side only, making it easy to simply tear out the pages and use as is, or if you choose you can cut out individual images to use on our own pages and projects. However, you'll probably want to use them again, so the enclosed CD-ROM contains all of the images individually as well as in the page layout form. The images are large enough to use at 12" x 12". Also included on the CDs are the actual fairy tale stories, in case we have used one you aren't familiar with. The CDs can be used with both PC and Mac formats. Just pop in the disk. On a PC, the file will immediately open to the Home page, which will walk you through how to view and print the images. For Macintosh users, you will simply double-click on the icon to open. The images may also be incorporated into your computer projects using simple imaging software that you can purchase specifically for this purpose—a perfect choice for digital scrapbooking.

The reference numbers printed on the back of each image in the book are the same ones used on the CD, which will allow you to easily find the image you are looking for. The numbering consists of the book abbreviation, the page number, the image number, and the file format. The first file number (located next to the page number) is for the entire page. For example, FTL01-01.jpg would be the entire image for page 1 of *Fairy Tales*. The second file number is for the top-right image. The numbers continue in a counterclockwise fashion. We have also included the name of the fairy tale on the back of each art page. There are a few art pages at the end of the book that are generic. Use these to "Create your own fairy tale."

Once you have resized your images, added text, created a scrapbook page, etc., you are ready to print them. Printing on cream or white cardstock, particularly a textured variety, creates a more authentic look. You won't be able to tell that it's a reproduction! If you don't have access to a computer or printer, that's ok. Most photocopy centers can resize and print your images for a nominal fee, or they have do-it-yourself machines that are easy to use.

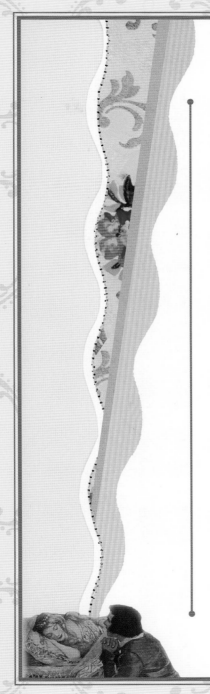

Ideas for Using the Images:

Scrapbooking: These images are perfect for both heritage and modern scrapbook pages. Simply use the image as a frame, accent piece, or border. For those of you with limited time, the page layouts in this book have been created so that you can use them as they are. Simply print out or photocopy the desired page, attach a photograph into one of the boxes, add your own journaling, and you have a beautiful designer scrapbook page in minutes. Be sure to print your images onto acid-free cardstock so the pages will last a lifetime.

Cards: Some computer programs allow images to be inserted into a card template, simplifying cardmaking. If this is not an option, simply use the images as accent pieces on the front or inside of the card. Use a bone folder to score the card's fold to create a more professional look.

Decoupage/Collage Projects: For decoupage or collage projects, photocopy or print the image onto a thinner paper such as copier paper. Thin paper adheres to projects more effectively. Decoupage medium glues and seals the project, creating a gloss or matte finish when dry, thus protecting the image. Vintage images are beautiful when decoupaged to cigar boxes, glass plates, and even wooden plaques. The possibilities are endless.

Fabric Arts: Vintage images can be used in just about any fabric craft imaginable: wall hangings, quilts, bags, or baby bibs. Either transfer the image onto the fabric by using a special iron-on paper, or by printing the image directly onto the fabric, using a temporary iron-on stabilizer that stabilizes the fabric to feed through a printer. These items are available at most craft and sewing stores. If the item will be washed, it is better to print directly on the fabric. For either method, follow the instructions on the package.

Wood Transfers: It is now possible to print images on wood. Use this exciting technique to create vintage plaques, clocks, frames, and more. A simple, inexpensive transfer tool is available at most large craft or home improvement stores, or online from various manufacturers. You simply place the photocopy of the image you want, face down, onto the surface and use the tool to transfer the image onto the wood. This process requires a copy from a laser printer, which means you will probably have to get your copies made at a copy center. Refer to manufacturer's instructions for additional details. There are other transfer products available that can be used with wood. Choose the one that is easiest for you.

Gallery of Ideas

These fairy tale images can be used in a variety of projects; cards, scrapbook pages, and decoupage projects to name a few. The images can be used as they are shown in the layout, or you can copy and clip out individual images, or even portions or multitudes of images. The following pages contain a collection of ideas to inspire you to use your imagination and create one-of-a-kind treasures.

art page 55

Idea 1

Use colors from this bright castles-and-forests border to stamp or write the photograph subject's name on a piece of cardstock. Glue the name to a corner and embellish with a button.

Justine Played Rapunzel in *Into the Woods* She Was so

A
Special Day
FOR JUSTINE
MAY 2005

Excited When the Big Night Came! She did A Great Job! The Whole Family came & Cheered Her on *We Love Our Star*

Idea 2   Add dimension by using foam dots to attach photographs, text, and images.

art page 39

Dainty little mermaid who lived under the sea

AthOLeen
and
HeR fellow
Mermaids
Circa
1938

had been wishing for many years

that a human she might be...

Idea 3 For journaling, try stamping your message with a variety of sizes and styles of alphabet stamps.

art page 25

She loved a prince with all her heart

& so she went one day, to see a wicked witch, who took her tail away...

ThE mermaids gather here

bathing

beauties

art page 26

Idea 4

If you want your photograph to fit behind an image on the page, simply cut away the background with a craft knife, then secure the image from behind.

Idea 5

This prince and princess fairy-tale wedding page is a perfect choice for scrapbooking that special wedding day. Add the wedding invitation and embellish with ribbons and a metal tag.

art page 50

Mr. and Mrs. Dee W. Wayment
request the pleasure of your company
at a wedding reception for their son,
Val E. Wayment
and
Suzanne Child
daughter of Mr. and Mrs. H. Roy Hansen
on Friday, May Twenty-first
nineteen hundred and sixty-five
from seven until ten in the evening
at the Ivy House
2408 Van Buren Ave.
Ogden, Utah

2 become 1

Idea 6

Glue small silver beads to the top of the photo and around the heart. Stamp or rub text onto the page, then adhere metal embellishments.

art page 51

Idea 7

Adhere a doily to the front of a card with temporary adhesive, then sew a straight stitch all around the card. Embellish with Cinderella image, rickrack, heart, words, and ribbon threaded through eyelets.

Idea 8

Glue patterned paper to cardstock, let dry, then use a pinwheel pattern to create a pinwheel. Glue ribbon around a painted dowel, then nail the pinwheel center to the dowel.

Idea 9
Remove the glass from a purchased frame and paint the frame. Hot-glue fabric to a piece of corkboard the size of the frame. Hot-glue bias tape diagonally across the board.

Idea 10
Print rabbit and garden images onto heavy cardstock and coat with decoupage medium for durability. Glue cabbage images onto thumbtacks.

FTL01-03   FTL01-02

FTL01-04

FTL01-01 • Aladdin

THE KING & QUEEN OF HEARTS

FTL02-02

FTL02-03

FTL02-08

FTL02-04   FTL02-09   FTL02-07

FTL02-05   FTL02-06

2   FTL02-01   Alice in Wonderland

FTL03-03   FTL03-02

FTL03-04   FTL03-05   FTL03-06

FTL03-01 • Alice in Wonderland

FTL04-04   FTL04-03   FTL04-02

            FTL04-08

                                      FTL04-07

FTL04-05   FTL04-06

FTL04-01 • Alice in Wonderland

FTL05-03

FTL05-02

FTL05-07

FTL05-04

FTL05-05

FTL05-06

FTL05-01 • Alice in Wonderland

FTL06-03   FTL06-02

                                              FTL06-06

                                       FTL06-05

                        FTL06-04

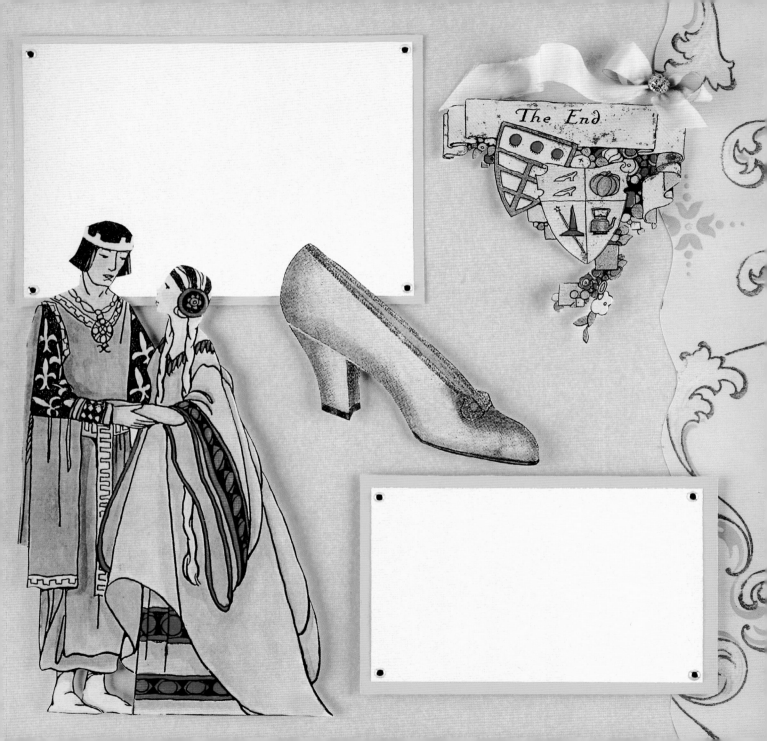

The End

FTL07-03   FTL07-02

                FTL07-08   FTL07-07

FTL07-04   FTL07-06

                FTL07-05

FTL07-01 • Cinderella

FTL08-03

FTL08-02

FTL08-04

FTL08-06

FTL08-05

FTL08-01 • Cinderella

FTL09-04   FTL09-03   FTL09-02

FTL09-05

                                                        FTL09-11
                    FTL09-12

FTL09-06   FTL09-07   FTL09-08   FTL09-09   FTL09-10

FTL09-01 • Cinderella

FTL10-02

FTL10-03

FTL10-04

FTL10-05   FTL10-06

FTL10-01 • Cinderella

FTL11-03

FTL11-02

FTL11-06

FTL11-04

FTL11-05

FTL11-01 • Cinderella

FTL12-03   FTL12-02

FTL12-04

                              FTL12-07

FTL12-05   FTL12-06

FTL12-01 • Cinderella

FTL13-03   FTL13-02

FTL13-04

FTL13-05   FTL13-07

FTL13-06

13 ┤ FTL13-01 • Cinderella

THE GINGERBREAD BOY

FTL14-03   FTL14-02

                                      FTL14-06

                                      FTL14-05

FTL14-04

FTL14-01 • The Gingerbread Boy

I am the gingerbread boy, I am, I am;
I can run from you, I can, I can!
I ran away from a little old woman,
A little old man,
A field full of mowers,
A barn full of threshers,
An old red cow,
A big fat pig,
And I can run from you, I can, I can!"

FTL15-03   FTL15-02

FTL15-04

FTL15-07

FTL15-05

FTL15-06

FTL15-01 • The Gingerbread Boy

Once upon a time there was

a little girl called

Goldilocks

because her curly hair

shone so brightly.....

While gathering flowers she happened on a

little cottage owned by three bears.

FTL16-04

FTL16-03

FTL16-02

FTL16-05

FTL16-08

FTL16-06

FTL16-07

FTL16-01 • Goldilocks and the Three Bears

"Somebody has been lying on my bed...

and there she is!"

Goldilocks was very frightened.

she jumped out of baby bears bed & ran out of the

cottage as fast as she could!

FTL17-02

FTL17-08

FTL17-03

FTL17-09   FTL17-07

FTL17-04

FTL17-05   FTL17-06

FTL17-01 • Goldilocks and the Three Bears

"Who has been

tasting my soup?"

"Who has been sitting in my chair?"

FTL18-03   FTL18-02

                        FTL18-08   FTL18-07

                                          FTL18-06

FTL18-04   FTL18-05

FTL18-01 • Goldilocks and the Three Bears

Goldilocks peeped in & found the place

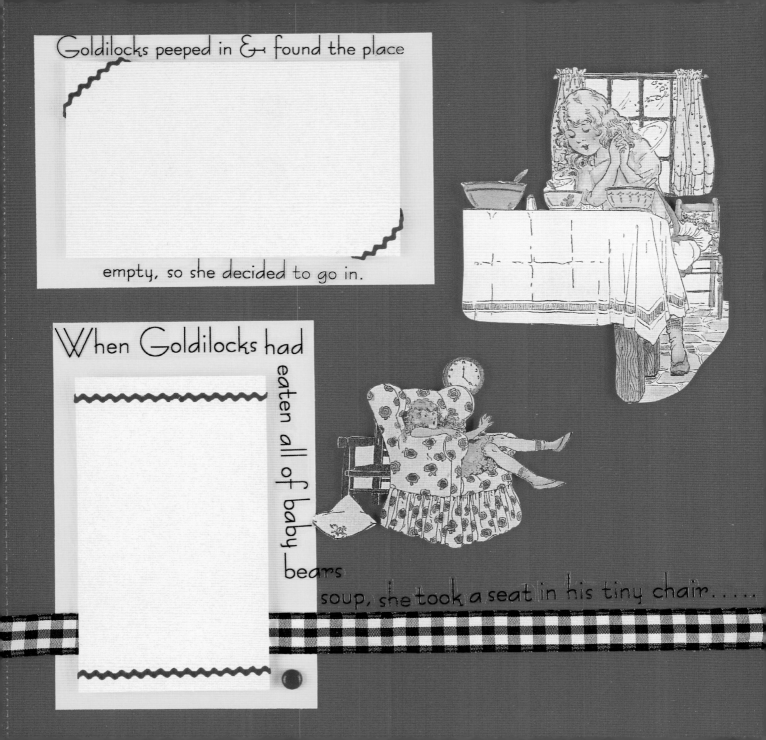

empty, so she decided to go in.

When Goldilocks had

eaten all of baby bears

soup, she took a seat in his tiny chair......

FTL19-02

FTL19-03

FTL19-06

FTL19-05

FTL19-04

FTL19-01 • Goldilocks and the Three Bears

FTL20-02

FTL20-03

FTL20-07

FTL20-04

FTL20-06

FTL20-05

20 — FTL20-01 • Hansel and Gretel

FTL21-03   FTL21-02

                    FTL21-06

FTL21-04   FTL21-05

JESSIE WILCOX SMITH

FTL22-04

FTL22-03

FTL22-02

FTL22-05

FTL22-06

FTL22-01 • Jack and the Beanstalk

FTL23-03

FTL23-02

FTL23-04

FTL23-08

FTL23-07

FTL23-05

FTL23-06

FTL23-01 • Jack and the Beanstalk

FTL24-03   FTL24-02

FTL24-04

FTL24-05   FTL24-06

FTL24-01 • Jack and the Beanstalk

A Dainty little mermaid who lived under the sea

had been wishing for many years

that a human she might be...

FTL25-03

FTL25-02

FTL25-04

FTL25-09

FTL25-05

FTL25-10

FTL25-08

FTL25-06

FTL25-07

FTL25-01 • The Little Mermaid

She loved a prince with all her heart

& so she went one day, to see a wicked witch, who took her tail away...

FTL26-02

FTL26-03

FTL26-04

FTL26-05

FTL26-06   FTL26-08

FTL26-07

FTL26-01 • The Little Mermaid

AYER'S HAIR VIGOR
FOR THE TOILET
Restores Gray Hair to its Natural Vitality and Color

PREPARED BY DR. J.C. AYER & CO. LOWELL MASS. U.S.A.

FTL27-03   FTL27-02

FTL27-04

FTL27-05

FTL27-06

FTL27-01 • The Little Mermaid

GRANDMA!

what sharp **TEETH** you have!

FTL28-03   FTL28-02

FTL28-08

FTL28-04   FTL28-07

FTL28-05   FTL28-06

FTL28-01 • Little Red Riding Hood

little
rEd
Riding hood

FTL29-03   FTL29-02

          FTL29-04   FTL29-09

FTL29-05

                                                              FTL29-08

FTL29-06   FTL29-07

FTL29-01 • Little Red Riding Hood

The lost boys begged
Wendy to be their
Mother.
They asked her to
Tuck them in at night,
And tell them stories
Before they went to bed....

FTL30-03

FTL30-02

FTL30-04

FTL30-01 • Peter Pan

"The crocodile!
The crocodile! "
Captain Hook
yelled, & in a
moment he was running
for his life...

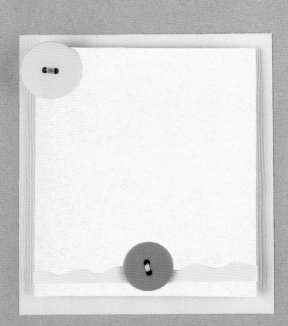

FTL31-03

FTL31-02

FTL31-04

FTL31-05

FTL31-01 • Peter Pan

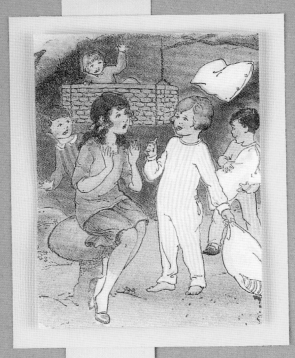

Mr. & Mrs. Darling had a nice maid, but the children were bathed & dressed by a big dog named Nana....

FTL32-03   FTL32-02

                                                FTL32-06

FTL32-04   FTL32-05

FTL32-01 • Peter Pan

FTL33-03   FTL33-02

                                                          FTL33-04

FTL33-01 • Peter Rabbit

FTL34-03   FTL34-02

FTL34-04   FTL34-05

FTL34-01 • Peter Rabbit

FTL35-03   FTL35-02

FTL35-04

FTL35-08

FTL35-05   FTL35-06   FTL35-07

FTL35-01 • Peter Rabbit

FTL36-03   FTL36-02

FTL36-04

FTL36-07

FTL36-05

FTL36-06

FTL36-01 • Peter Rabbit

FTL37-04   FTL37-03   FTL37-02

FTL37-05

FTL37-06   FTL37-07

FTL37-01 • The Frog Prince

FTL38-02

FTL38-03   FTL38-06

FTL38-04   FTL38-05

FTL38-01 • The Frog Prince

FTL39-03

FTL39-02

FTL39-04

FTL39-05

FTL39-06

FTL39-01 • Rapunzel

A Sleep that was to last one Hundred Years

first

KISS

FTL40-03   FTL40-02

                                                      FTL40-04

FTL40-01 • Sleeping Beauty

The Kingdom in which the
little Princess was born was
a Favorite Dwelling Place
for Fairies

baby

P R I N C E S S

FTL41-03   FTL41-02

FTL41-04
                    FTL41-08

                    FTL41-09

FTL41-05
                                            FTL41-07

FTL41-06

FTL41-01 • Sleeping Beauty

FTL42-03

FTL42-02

FTL42-04   FTL42-05

FTL42-06

FTL42-01 • Sleeping Beauty

FTL43-03   FTL43-02

                                    FTL43-06

FTL43-04

                    FTL43-05

FTL43-01 • Sleeping Beauty

FTL44-03   FTL44-02

FTL44-04   FTL44-05

FTL44-01 • Sleeping Beauty

FTL45-03   FTL45-02

                                                                        FTL45-06

FTL45-04

                                                                        FTL45-05

FTL45-01 • Snow White

FTL46-04　　　　　　　　FTL46-03　　　　　　　　FTL46-02

FTL46-05　　　　　　　　FTL46-06

FTL46-01 • Snow White

FTL47-02

FTL47-03

FTL47-04

FTL47-01 • Snow White and Rose Red

TOM THUMB

DON'T FALL
INTO THE
PUDDING!

FL

FTL48-03   FTL48-02

        FTL48-04

FTL48-05

FTL48-06   FTL48-07   FTL48-08

FTL48-01 • Tom Thumb

FTL49-03

FTL49-02

FTL49-08

FTL49-04

FTL49-07

FTL49-05

FTL49-06

FTL49-01 • Tom Thumb

FTL50-04   FTL50-03   FTL50-02

                                                         FTL50-07

        FTL50-05   FTL50-06

FTL50-01 • **Create your own fairy tale.** • *. . . And they lived happily ever after.*

FTL51-02

FTL51-03

FTL51-04

FTL51-01 • **Create your own fairy tale.** • . . . *And they lived happily ever after.*

«Il y avait une fois..

FTL52-03   FTL52-02

FTL52-04   FTL52-06

FTL52-05

FTL52-01 • Create your own fairy tale. • *Court Jester*

FTL53-02

FTL53-03

FTL53-01 • Create your own fairy tale. • *Fairies*

FTL54-03

FTL54-01 • **Create your own fairy tale.** • *Fairies and Pirates*

FTL55-02

FTL55-03

FTL55-01 • Create your own fairy tale. • *Once upon a time . . .*

PLAYFUL

PIXIES

FTL56-03

FTL56-02

FTL56-04

FTL56-06

FTL56-05

FTL56-01 • Create your own fairy tale. • *Pixies*

FTL57-03

FTL57-02

FTL57-04

FTL57-05

FTL57-01 • Create your own fairy tale. • *Pixies*